Comprehension Success

Success

3

James Driver

Oxford University Press

Preface

Comprehension is a comprehensive activity that involves many different aspects of English. This book uses the traditional role of comprehension – asking questions on the content of short texts – as a starting-point from which to investigate, in depth, a variety of different kinds of writing.

The thirty double-pages of comprehensions offer a wide variety of texts – examples from information books, action rhymes, realia such as postcards and notices, children's fiction, fable, catalogues, comic strips, picture books, poems and legends – a whole range of genres, drawn from authentic texts.

The pupils are then encouraged to use a range of strategies to discover meaning. They will practise locating, selecting, collating, identifying, using, retrieving, examining and re-presenting ideas and information, and, by employing quotation, deduction and inference, find that their confidence as readers who fully appreciate a text will continue to grow.

There are three sections on most of the question pages. Section A contains the most straightforward recall questions. The questions in Section B often call for a deeper insight into the nature of the text. The knowledge gained from answering one, or both, of these two sets of questions is used in Section C, which offers a prompt for a creative writing activity, in the same genre as the selected text.

The confidence that comes from being able to understand the main points about the facts, characters and events that appear in a broad range of texts encourages readers to read more widely and enables them to gain a better understanding of how writing, its form, language and content, works. This, in turn, should lead to a faster development of their ability as writers.

OXFORD
UNIVERSITY PRESS

Great Clarendon Street, Oxford OX2 6DP

Oxford University Press is a department of the University of Oxford
It furthers the University's objective of excellence in research, scholarship, and education by publishing worldwide in

Oxford New York

Auckland Cape Town Dar es Salaam Hong Kong Karachi
Kuala Lumpur Madrid Melbourne Mexico City Nairobi
New Delhi Shanghai Taipei Toronto

With offices in

Argentina Austria Brazil Chile Czech Republic France Greece
Guatemala Hungary Italy Japan Poland Portugal Singapore
South Korea Switzerland Thailand Turkey Ukraine Vietnam

Oxford is a registered trade mark of Oxford University Press
in the UK and in certain other countries

© Oxford University Press 1998
First published 1998
20 19 18 17 16 15 14 13 12
ISBN-13: 978-0-19-834180-2
ISBN 0 19 834180 6

Typeset and designed by Oxford Designers & Illustrators.

Printed in Thailand by Imago

Contents

The honeybee

This page is taken from a science information book.

A closer look

This picture shows a honeybee ten times bigger than in real life. You can see the different parts of its body.

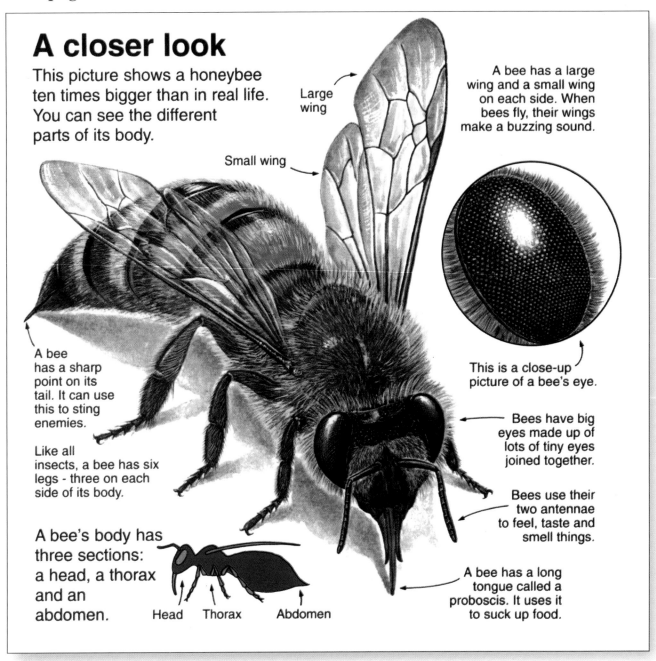

Large wing

Small wing

A bee has a large wing and a small wing on each side. When bees fly, their wings make a buzzing sound.

A bee has a sharp point on its tail. It can use this to sting enemies.

Like all insects, a bee has six legs - three on each side of its body.

This is a close-up picture of a bee's eye.

Bees have big eyes made up of lots of tiny eyes joined together.

Bees use their two antennae to feel, taste and smell things.

A bee's body has three sections: a head, a thorax and an abdomen.

Head   Thorax   Abdomen

A bee has a long tongue called a proboscis. It uses it to suck up food.

A

1 How many wings does a bee have?

2 On which section of the bee's body would you find the wings?

3 How many legs does a bee have?

4 On which section of a bee's body would you find the legs?

5 Which is the longest section of the bee's body?

6 What does a bee use when it has to defend itself?

7 Which parts of the bee make the buzzing sound?

B

1 Write down the word used on the opposite page that means a **bee's tongue**.

2 Write down the word used on the opposite page that makes it clear bees **don't** chew their food.

3 **a)** Are bees able to smell the flowers they land on?
   b) Give a good reason based on the information on the opposite page.

4 **a)** Do bees have powerful eyes?
   b) Give a good reason based on the information on the opposite page.

C

Much of the information on the opposite page is given to you by **captions**.

A **caption** is a label which explains a picture with a sentence or two of text. On the picture of the honeybee the **captions** have arrows pointing to the parts of the bee they are explaining.

Make an outline drawing of your classroom. Add written **captions** to explain the **purpose** of each extra object in the classsroom.

The human ear

This page is also from a science information book.

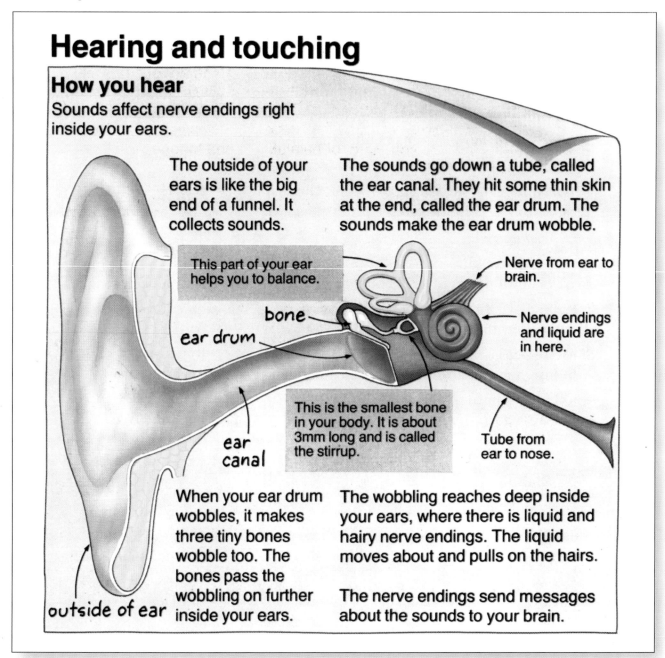

Hearing and touching

How you hear
Sounds affect nerve endings right inside your ears.

The outside of your ears is like the big end of a funnel. It collects sounds.

The sounds go down a tube, called the ear canal. They hit some thin skin at the end, called the ear drum. The sounds make the ear drum wobble.

This part of your ear helps you to balance.

Nerve from ear to brain.

bone

Nerve endings and liquid are in here.

ear drum

This is the smallest bone in your body. It is about 3mm long and is called the stirrup.

ear canal

Tube from ear to nose.

When your ear drum wobbles, it makes three tiny bones wobble too. The bones pass the wobbling on further inside your ears.

The wobbling reaches deep inside your ears, where there is liquid and hairy nerve endings. The liquid moves about and pulls on the hairs.

outside of ear

The nerve endings send messages about the sounds to your brain.

1 What job does the **outside** of the ear do?

2 What is the name given to the channel that connects the outer ear to the inner ear?

3 What is the ear drum made out of?

4 What happens to the ear drum when a sound hits it?

5 What carries the sound from the ear drum further on into the ear?

6 What does the liquid pull and move around?

1 What is special about the **stirrup**?

2 Where do the nerves take their messages?

3 It allows you to hear, but what else does the inner ear help you to do?

4 Why do you think the ear drum and the tiny bones are so far **inside** the head?

Imagine you hear a loud noise, like an explosion. Write in your own words all the stages the sound goes through, before your brain understands that it has heard a loud bang.

Snakes

This page is from a fact book on snakes.

SNAKES AND PEOPLE

Snakes have been given a bad name for years because a small number of species cause many human deaths. Over 10,000 people die from snake-bite poisoning every year.

The main killer snakes are Indian cobras and Russell's and saw-scaled vipers in India; pit vipers, rattlesnakes and coral snakes in South America; puff adders, Egyptian cobras and saw-scaled vipers in Africa; tiger and brown snakes in Australia; and the diamondback rattlesnakes in the United States.

▼ Snake charmers perform on the streets of some Asian and African countries. Cobras are often used in these acts, but their fangs are removed so that they cannot inject their powerful poisons.

IF YOU ARE IN SNAKE COUNTRY . . .

Wear shoes, socks and trousers.

Do not poke around under rocks, logs and other places where snakes might be hiding.

Do not go out without an adult.

IF YOU ARE LUCKY ENOUGH TO SEE A SNAKE . . .

Remember that although most snakes are harmless you should not touch them.

Stand still and allow it to slide away to safety.

IF YOU ARE EVER BITTEN BY A SNAKE TELL AN ADULT AS SOON AS POSSIBLE

A

1 Why are people afraid of snakes?

2 Name **two** countries where cobras live.

3 Write down the words used in the first paragraph that tell you that not all snakes are dangerous.

4 Many of the dangerous snakes have very descriptive names. How do you think you would recognise a **diamondback** rattlesnake?

5 Why is the snake charmer in the picture not in danger?

6 What is the correct name for the teeth a snake uses to inject its poison?

B

1 Why, when you are in snake country, do you think you should wear strong shoes, thick socks and trousers?

2 Name **two** places where snakes like to rest.

3 The instructions tell you to **stand still** if you see a snake. What does this tell you about the way snakes find their prey?

4 Why do you think people want to watch snake charmers?

5 Write down the word used in the instructions that describes the way snakes move.

C

The pictures and words inside the box give you clear **instructions** about what you should do in snake country.

Make a similar set of **instructions** telling someone what they should do if they found themselves in **one** of the following situations:

a) If they are crossing a road by your school.

b) If they find a fire in the school.

c) If they find a suspicious package on the train.

Amazing creatures

This page is from an encyclopedia.

Pouncing puma
Pumas are very agile. They bound from rock to rock, pounce on their prey and spring up into trees. They can cover 18 metres in a single leap. Most pumas now live in the western part of America.

A fantastic leap
The common flea, a tiny wingless insect, can jump 20 centimetres into the air. This means it jumps more than 130 times its own height. Fleas jump on to animals to feed on their blood.

Champion Jumpers

In a high jump or long jump contest between animals and humans, there is no doubt who would win. The highest any athlete has ever jumped is less than 2.4 metres, but kangaroos, and even the Goliath frog can clear 3 metres. The human world record for long jump stands at under 9 metres, while the puma leaps 18 metres at a time. If a man could jump as high as a flea in comparison to his height, he would clear the tallest office block in Great Britain.
Animals that glide have no real human equivalent. They include the flying squirrels with their wing-like flaps of skin, and the flying fishes with their extra large fins. Each glide may last hundreds of metres.

Jumping giant
Frogs have strong back legs for jumping. The biggest frog in the world, the Goliath frog, is also the best high-jumper. It can leap 3 metres into the air. In America, competitions are held to find the best long-jumping frogs.

Unique glider
A few animals, like the flying squirrel, have a flap of skin between their front and back legs which helps them glide from tree to tree. The colugo has a bigger cloak of skin, and it can glide twice as far – up to 100 metres.

A

1 Why do fleas need to jump?

2 Why can't fleas fly?

3 Write down **two** words used in the piece on the puma that mean **jump**.

4 Why do pumas need to be able to jump so far?

5 The Goliath Frog is a **double** record-breaker!
What are the **two** records the Goliath Frog holds?

6 What is unusual about the **colugo**?

7 Why is the Goliath Frog able to jump so far?

B

1 Why can the colugo glide twice as far as the flying squirrel?

2 **a)** Find another creature mentioned on the opposite page, not the colugo or the flying squirrel, that also glides.
   b) What does this creature use in place of the cloak of skin?

3 **a)** Which one of the animals on the opposite page do you think would be the most difficult to keep as a pet?
   b) Give **two** good reasons to explain why this animal would cause more problems than the others.

C

You are the main **commentator** at the Animal Olympics. It is your job to tell the people watching the events on television exactly what is happening and especially who is winning!

1 Write down what you would say in the **commentary** for the long jump.
There are three competitors: a puma, a human and a flying squirrel.

2 Write down what you would say in the **commentary** for the high jump.
There are three competitors: a flea, a Goliath Frog and a human.

Mustard and cress

These are instructions from a children's gardening book.

Mustard and Cress

You can begin your gardening by sowing mustard and cress which grows very quickly. You will enjoy eating it all the more because you have grown it yourself!

You Will Need

Dinner plates

Several squares of absorbent kitchen paper

A packet each of mustard and cress seeds

1 Place the paper on a dinner plate and wet it well with water. Pour away the excess water.

2 Sprinkle some cress seeds quite thinly on one half of the paper, making sure no seeds lie on top of each other.

3 Cover your seeds with a dry square of paper or place another plate over the top, to keep out the light until the tiny roots and shoots start to grow.

4 Three days later, sow the mustard seeds on the other half of the paper. Mustard germinates more quickly than cress, so they will be ready to cut at the same time. Keep the paper moist but not soaking wet. Cover again.

5 When the cress is about 1.3 cm ($\frac{1}{2}$ in.) high, uncover and place the plate on a sunny window-sill. Don't forget to keep the paper moist. Let your crop grow to about 7.5 cm (3 in.) high when it will be ready to harvest.

6 Cut with scissors and eat in sandwiches or salad. If your family likes your home-grown salad keep up the supply! One packet of both mustard and cress seeds will give several crops.

A

1 What condition must the paper be in **before** you sow the seeds?

2 Why do you sow the cress seeds **before** the mustard seeds?

3 What **two** things should have appeared on the cress seeds before you allow them into the light?

4 What is the difference between **moist** and **soaking**?

5 How do you make sure the young plants get plenty of light?

6 What do you use to harvest your crop?

7 Name the **two** different ways the instructions suggest that mustard and cress should be eaten.

8 Find the word in instruction 1 that means **extra**.

9 Find the word in instruction 4 that means **puts out shoots**.

B

1 **a)** Do you think growing mustard and cress is a project that could be done by your class?

   b) Give a good reason to support your answer.

2 What **doesn't** mustard and cress need that most other plants do need?

3 Which instruction is repeated more than any other?

C

Is there something simple you know how to cook? Or a model you know how to make? Write out the instructions, and draw some simple diagrams, using the layout opposite as a model.

Baked potatoes

These instructions are from a children's cookery book.

Using an oven

Most ovens need time to heat up, so you need to turn them on before you start cooking. To do this, turn the oven knob to the temperature given in the recipe. Usually, this makes a light come on which goes out when the oven is hot enough. Remember that if you have a fan oven it may be different, so check in your instruction book.

Baked potatoes

For two potatoes you will need:
2 large baking potatoes
cooking oil
butter or margarine

For the fillings, choose:
200g (7oz) tin tuna
1 tbs mayonnaise
200g (7oz) tin sweetcorn
or:
75g (3oz) cheese
pickle

stiff brush for cleaning potatoes, fork, kitchen paper, baking tray, oven gloves, kitchen knife, tin opener, tablespoon, small bowl, grater, plate, teaspoon

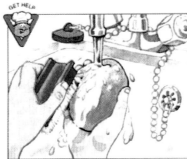

Turn the oven on to 200°C (400°F, Gas Mark 6). Scrub the potatoes with the brush in cold water.

Prick the potatoes all over with a fork. Wipe on some oil with kitchen paper. Put them onto a baking tray.

Put the tray of potatoes into the oven. Cook them for about one hour, then take them out carefully.

Test the potatoes with a kitchen knife. If they are cooked, they will feel soft all the way through.

If they are still hard, cook them for another 30 minutes and test them again. If they are soft, cut them in half.

Put a little butter or margarine into each potato. Put the filling you have chosen on top (see right).

A

1 When you bake potatoes should you leave the skin on or take it off?

2 What is the oven doing while you are scrubbing the potatoes?

3 **a)** How long do you keep the potatoes in the oven before you take them out for the first time?

   b) Why does the recipe tell you to take them out **carefully**?

4 **a)** What do you use a **fork** for when you are baking potatoes?

   b) What do you use a **knife** for when you are baking potatoes?

5 When do you cut the potatoes in half?

6 List three different ingredients the recipe suggests for fillings.

B

Four of the pictures in the recipe have a little **icon** in the top left hand corner. The **icon** is there to remind you about important things.

1 What is the picture on the icon that warns you about the oven being hot?

2 Why do you think the icon that reminds you to **take care** has a picture of two knives on it?

3 What is the circle in the centre of the **turn it off** icon meant to be?

4 **a)** The **get help** icon appears in the first picture. What part of the instructions that appear with that picture do you think you should **get help** with?

   b) Why do you think you need to **get help** with this?

C

An **icon** is a quick pictorial way of sending a message.

Design a set of three **icons** to go in a car.

The first **icon** is to remind people that they must put on their seat belts.

The second is to tell people not to stick their heads out of the windows.

The third is to remind the driver to look out for children.

Day trip

An advertisement for a school outing.

AS LOW AS £19 PER HEAD

A REAL EDUCATIONAL TRIP

A GREAT DAY OUT IN FRANCE via THE CHANNEL TUNNEL
With *le Shuttle*

6 HOURS IN FRANCE

IDEAL FOR ALL AGES

BOULOGNE

Dear Head Teacher

Why not organise a DAY-TRIP for a group from your school this year and experience the marvel of the CHANNEL TUNNEL? The speed of the crossing (35 minutes) means that DAY-TRIPS are now entirely feasible for all schools situated south of Birmingham and east of Bristol. The cost can be AS LOW AS £19 PER HEAD (see below). One of our LUXURY COACHES will collect your group early in the morning and drive to Folkestone. A suggested itinerary might then be:

10.30am	Arrive Channel Tunnel Terminal at Folkestone
11.00am	Le Shuttle leaves Folkestone
12.35pm (local time)	Le Shuttle arrives Calais
12.35pm - 6.45pm	Free time for visits to Calais, Boulogne, Cité Europe
	Coach available for use throughout visit
6.45pm	Check in for return journey
7.15pm	Le Shuttle leaves Calais Terminal
6.50pm (local time)	Le Shuttle arrives Folkestone Terminal, Return home

N.B. This is only a suggested itinerary. You are quite free to shorten or lengthen your visit as you think fit (subject to a maximum total duration time of 20 hours). You may also take the ferry from Dover to Calais if you prefer.

COST: £950 for a 49 seater luxury coach (with video and seat belts). *Add £100 if you are more than 300km from Folkestone (north of Birmingham, west of Bristol). Add £100 if you wish to travel on a Saturday.*

BOOKING: All you have to do is **telephone 01295 721717** or **fax us 01295 721991** with a suggested date. We shall then send you:-
- A detailed itinerary with all the necessary reservations.
- Suggestions of what to do and where to go.

- A checklist for your trip, (including the guide *Ma Visite en France*).
- Collective passport information.
- An invoice for £100 deposit to confirm the booking; **repayable in full** if trip is cancelled more than 2 months before departure; balance due 4 weeks before departure.

Please contact Colin Galloway or Jackie Bradley for any further information on 01295 721717
We look forward to hearing from you.

SAGTA
School & Group Travel Assoc.

DRAGONS INTERNATIONAL *in conjunction with* *le Shuttle*

ABTA

Dragons International, Godswell House, Bloxham, Banbury, OX15 4ES **Telephone 01295 721717**

V 8389

A

1 Which country does the advert say you will visit?

2 How will you travel to Folkestone?

3 How will you cross the Channel?

4 Which town will you arrive at on the other side?

5 What is the name of the company that will organize your trip?

6 How long will you be able to spend abroad?

B

1 a) Will it cost more to go on the trip if you live **north** of Birmingham or **south** of Birmingham?

   b) Why do you think it costs more if you live there?

2 What information does an **itinerary** tell you?

3 What is the title of the guidebook the travel company give you?

4 What do the initials **S.A.G.T.A** stand for?

5 Explain how, according to the timetable, the school trip will arrive back in England **before** it has left France!

6 a) Would you like to travel on the coach?

   b) Give a good reason to explain why you feel like this.

7 What do you think would be the worst part of this trip? Explain why.

C

Imagine some children from another country are planning to spend a day with you. Because they are on a day trip they will only be able to spend 6 hours with you. They will arrive at 11.00 am and leave at 5.00 pm.

They want to learn as much as they can about the way you live: where you go to school, what you eat, how you amuse yourself, what games you play, where you play, what sort of shops you go to, the different jobs that people do who live near you, the pets that people keep – everything!

Write out a **timetable** for their day. Try to give them enough time to discover as much as they can about as many different things as they can.

Poetry competition

This competition is from a magazine produced by a bookshop for its young readers.

12 POETRY IN MOTION

POETRY PLEASE

RHYME'S REASON

Earlier this year, Dillons and the children's newspaper, *Young Telegraph* teamed up to run a competition to find ten judges between the ages of eight and 14 to judge a selection of the best poetry books for children. To be chosen, they had to send in a poem of their own. There were an incredible 7,000 entries from which the ten winners were selected.

Not only did the winners get to judge Dillons Top Poetry Books, but they were also treated to a VIP day out at Dillons in Nottingham. Each winner then got to choose £100 worth of books from the huge selection in the new children's department!

Over the next few issues of *Word Up*, we will publish some of the winning judges poems.

Craig Stephens, David McIntyre, Lisa MacDonald, Ruth Jones, Sarah Haines, John Gethin, Hannah Gethin, Krystal Georgiou, Stefan Episkopou with staff from Dillons of Nottingham.

The Fidgiebray

No one knows because I don't say,
I'm secretly a Fidgiebray.
I sit at the back of the class near the wall,
I'm a hairy green monster eight feet tall.
Oh the joys of giving my class mates a scare,
by waving my tentacles in the air,
A whole sixteen I had last night,
Each one green and slimy a horrible sight.
Thanks to my eight emerald eyes all oozing with slime
I can write out four maths questions at one time.
I listen to my teacher give us a talk,
Oh no! My belly button's gone for a walk.
"Stop!" I cry, but oh it's too late,
My belly button has met its fate.
It climbs up our terrible teacher Miss Strouse,
"Eek!" She cries, "I think it's a mouse."
She runs out of the room. I observe with eight eyes,
"Class dismissed!" she quickly cries.
And so there goes another day,
In my secret life as a Fidgiebray.

by John Gethin, age 11

Crack Another Yolk

compiled by John Foster

Get your tonsils in a twist with this brilliant new book of word play poems. Packed with puns, jokes, riddles, limericks and acrostics – words will never sound the same again.

£7.99 hbk
£3.99 pbk
Oxford

The New Gnus

by John Foster

A gnu who was,
new to the zoo

Asked another gnu what
he should do.

The other gnu said, shaking
his head,

If I knew, I'd tell you,
I'm new too.

Jenny Morris

Wondercrump Poetry!

by children for children

It's back. The third book of weird and wacky Wondercrump Poetry is packed with prize-winning poems for children by children. All the children entered the annual Roald Dahl poetry competition. Is the next Roald Dahl lurking in these pages? Read it and see!

£3.50 *Red Fox*

IT'S RATHER DARK IN HERE

I am writing these
lines from inside a lion
And it's rather dark in here!
So excuse the writing that
may not be too clear
But I am afraid to tell you
last night I got too near.

Oliver Oldman (7)
Gerrards Cross School
Buckinghamshire

All proceeds go to the Roald Dahl Foundation. For your entry form please write to Wondercrump, Random House Children's Books, 20 Vauxhall Bridge Road, London SW1V 2SA.

A

1 What is the name of the bookshop that organised this competition?

2 **a)** How many people entered the competition?
   b) Who was allowed to enter the competition?

3 **a)** How many winners were there?
   b) What did the winners have to do to win?
   c) What job were the winners asked to do?

4 **a)** Where did the winners go?
   b) What extra prize did the winners receive?

5 Write down the title of one of the winning poems.

6 What is the name of the magazine in which this article appeared?

B

1 Find the name of a **different** poetry competition that is featured on this page.

2 What is the name of the book in which the winning poems of this competition appear?

3 **a)** Write down the name of one of the prize-winners in this competition.
   b) What was his poem about?

4 Find the poem written by Jenny Morris. It is a shape poem. What are the words supposed to look like?

5 Find the word used in the information about the poetry books that means "collected".

C

Think of a prize you would like your class to win. It can be anything that will help your education – a swimming pool to use in PE, an aeroplane to take you on Geography trips, a theatre in which you can perform your drama, a time machine to help you with your History – anything!

When you have thought of the prize invent the **competition** that the schools wanting to win the prize would have to enter. Because your prize is such an amazing prize your competition should be a real challenge for all the schools taking part. Write a letter that explains what the competitors have to do to win and lists the rules that they will have to follow.

How computers work

This diagram is from the *Oxford Children's Pocket Book of Knowledge*.

Computers

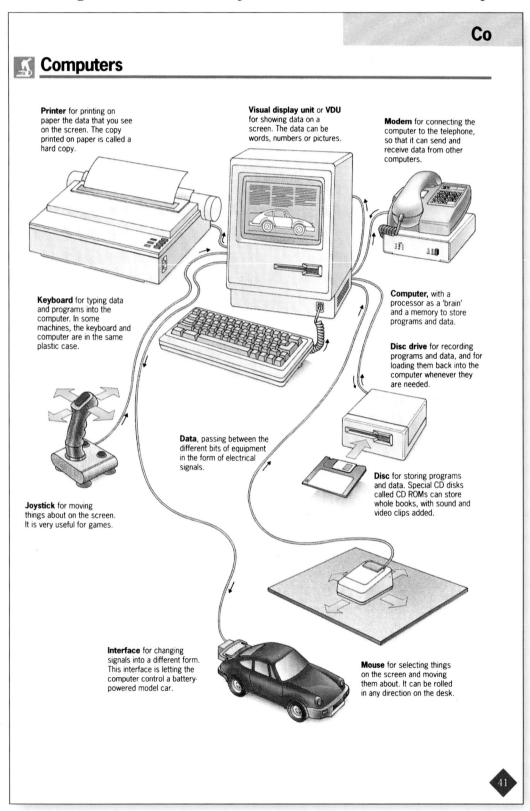

Printer for printing on paper the data that you see on the screen. The copy printed on paper is called a hard copy.

Visual display unit or **VDU** for showing data on a screen. The data can be words, numbers or pictures.

Modem for connecting the computer to the telephone, so that it can send and receive data from other computers.

Keyboard for typing data and programs into the computer. In some machines, the keyboard and computer are in the same plastic case.

Computer, with a processor as a 'brain' and a memory to store programs and data.

Disc drive for recording programs and data, and for loading them back into the computer whenever they are needed.

Data, passing between the different bits of equipment in the form of electrical signals.

Disc for storing programs and data. Special CD disks called CD ROMs can store whole books, with sound and video clips added.

Joystick for moving things about on the screen. It is very useful for games.

Interface for changing signals into a different form. This interface is letting the computer control a battery-powered model car.

Mouse for selecting things on the screen and moving them about. It can be rolled in any direction on the desk.

41

1 What do the letters **VDU** stand for?

2 What piece of equipment do you need to send data by telephone from one computer to another computer?

3 Write down the names of **two** pieces of equipment that can move things around on the screen.

4 What can be stored on a **disc**?

5 What do you call the piece of equipment **discs** are put into?

6 What piece of equipment is used to type data into the computer?

Computers deal with information. This information is called **data**.

1 Write down **three** different sorts of data that a computer can show you.

2 What does a computer need to store its data?

3 Which part of the computer turns data into **hard copy**?

4 What form does the data take when it is travelling between the different pieces of computer equipment?

5 What part of the computer is like a human's brain?

The opposite page contains a great deal of information. It is divided into short passages of text that are put next to the related parts of the diagram.

Draw a diagram of a petrol station, with all the things you have to do to get petrol.

Next to each part of the picture write a short piece of text, no more than **15** words long, that explains as clearly as possible exactly what that part of the picture is there for.

An illumination

An illumination is a small picture, painted by hand, that was used to decorate books before the invention of printing.

This is the illumination for the month of October from the Book of Hours, *Les Très Riches Heures du Duc de Berry.* The Duc de Berry was a great collector and patron of the arts in 15th-century France. He commissioned the illustrations for this book from the Limbourg brothers, three well known young artists who worked together on illuminations (and who all died before they were 30).

The scene is just outside Paris. In the background is the palace of the Louvre (as it then was). The man in red is riding a horse, which is drawing a harrow to break up the ground. The one in blue carries a sling full of seed, and is sowing it by hand. The figure in the middle is not an archer practising, but a scarecrow! (Today scarecrows have sticks or guns, but then they had bows.)

The artist has shown the men's bodies moving naturally, as they set about their tasks. But there are other interesting 'natural' points about this picture. Look at the figures again. You'll see that they cast shadows, even the tiny figures in the background, and that the boat on the river is reflected in the water. Nothing very special about that, we think. But this small picture (almost the same size as on this page) is the oldest example we know of an artist showing shadows and reflections. It was the start of looking at light in a different way.

October', from 'Les Très Riches Heures du Duc de Berry', a 15th–century manuscript.

1 Who first owned the book this illumination comes from?

2 Who painted the pictures in this book?

3 What was rather sad about the lives of these painters?

4 In which country was this picture painted?

5 What job is the man on the horse doing?

6 What job is the person carrying the bow doing?

7 a) What do you think the birds at the bottom left of the picture are eating?
b) Where has this food come from?

1 Look very carefully at the middle part of the picture. How do the people get down from the river bank and into the boats?

2 What do you think the top, curved part of the picture was used for?

3 This is a very important picture in the history of art because it is the first time artists tried to show **exactly** how light affects the way we see things. Write down **two** things the artists put in this picture that had never been painted before.

4 Why do you think there is a stone on the harrow?

Which one of the people in the picture would you like to be?

Give a good reason to explain why you have chosen this person.

Then write a paragraph about how you think they spent their day. Refer to details in the picture, as much as you can.

A medieval feast

This page is from a history book, describing customs in about the year 1240.

Having a Feast

The 'kitchen' is just a group of sheds in the courtyard. Servants have been working here since dawn.

Spices and herbs must be ground up with a mortar and pestle. Lots of spices are used, to hide the taste of the meat. Without refrigerators, it goes bad quickly.

Much of the meat is roasted on spits in front of the fire. The servant boy who has to turn this spit is using an old, wet archery target as a fire screen.

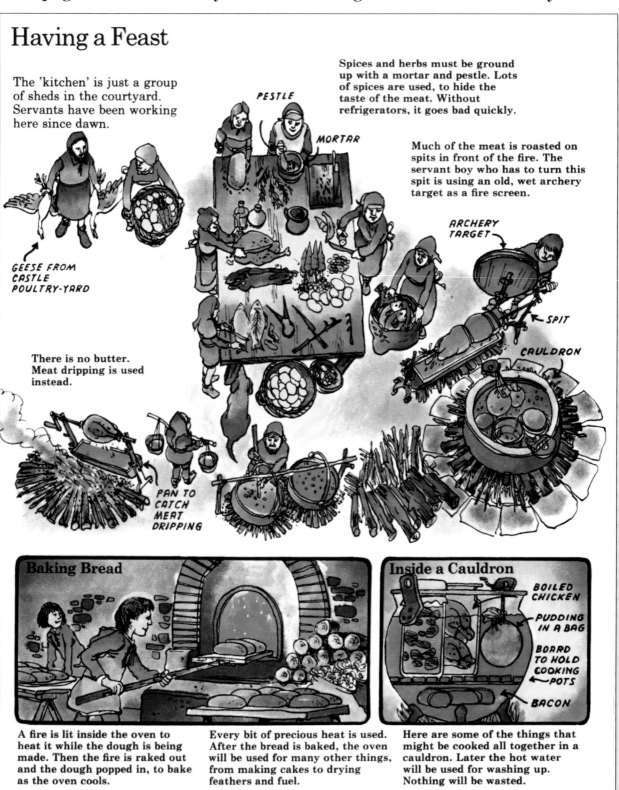

PESTLE

MORTAR

GEESE FROM CASTLE POULTRY-YARD

ARCHERY TARGET

SPIT

CAULDRON

There is no butter. Meat dripping is used instead.

PAN TO CATCH MEAT DRIPPING

Baking Bread

A fire is lit inside the oven to heat it while the dough is being made. Then the fire is raked out and the dough popped in, to bake as the oven cools.

Every bit of precious heat is used. After the bread is baked, the oven will be used for many other things, from making cakes to drying feathers and fuel.

Inside a Cauldron

BOILED CHICKEN

PUDDING IN A BAG

BOARD TO HOLD COOKING POTS

BACON

Here are some of the things that might be cooked all together in a cauldron. Later the hot water will be used for washing up. Nothing will be wasted.

1 In a medieval kitchen, what was a **spit** used for?

2 Why does someone have to keep turning the **spit**?

3 What is the boy turning the **spit** using the archery target for?

4 What is the giant cooking pot called?

5 How do you think meat **dripping** got its name?

1 You are asked to grind up some big lumps of salt. You are given a **pestle** and **mortar**.
   a) Explain clearly what you would do with the **pestle**.
   b) Explain clearly what you would use the **mortar** for.

2 Why were cauldrons so big?

3 Here are the 6 steps that bakers followed when they were making bread. Copy them out in the **right order**.
Bake the bread. Put the bread in. Take the bread out. Light the fire. Make the dough. Rake out the fire.

4 In the picture lots of strong tasting spices and herbs are being used to cook the meat. What does this tell you about the condition of the meat?

5 Read the captions to the bottom two pictures carefully.
   a) Name **two** things that weren't wasted by the cooks in ancient times.
   b) What does this tell you about the fuel they used in those days?

There is a great deal of information on the opposite page. Some of it is in words, some of it is in pictures.

Using as much of this information as you can, see if you can write out the **menu** for the great feast that the cooks and their helpers are preparing.

Put in as much information as you can about all the different foods that are being prepared.

A coat of arms

This page is from a history book about heraldry.

The knight's body is covered with mail, which is like a garment knitted not with wool but with steel. Over it he wears a loose coat called the coat-armour, which helped to protect him from sword-blows. On his head is a helmet with a piece of metal coming down over his nose. This guarded his nose, but it also made it hard to be sure who he was, because his face could not be seen properly.

You can imagine how difficult it was for the king to tell who the leaders were, for the leaders to know each other, and for the soldiers to know their own lord!

How would you mark the knights so that all would know who was who? Would you write their names on their coat-armour? That would not do because few people – even important people – could read in those days.

In fact what the knights did was to paint a bold and bright shape, or design, on their shields, and also on their coat-armour, flags, and horse-covering. They did this so that everyone could tell who they were, even from a long way away. Because these designs were painted on their coat-armour they came to be called "coats of arms", or just "arms".

A

1 What was the **mail** a knight wore made from?

2 As well as mail, knights wore other things to protect themselves.
Write down **two** other things a knight wore to protect himself in battle.

3 Why was it difficult to see a knight's face when he was dressed for battle?

4 Why didn't the knights **write** their names on their coat-armour?

5 Make a list of **three** different things belonging to a knight that might show his coat of arms.

6 Why did the knights use such bright colours in their coats of arms?

B

1 Write down the word used in the first sentence that means **a piece of clothing**.

2 Write down a word used in the second sentence that **is** a piece of clothing.

3 Write down **three** different words used in the second paragraph that are all names given to people in charge of other people.

4 Find the word in the third paragraph that means a garment, or a piece of clothing.

5 The word **arms** appears in the last paragraph. What does it mean?

C

The knight in the picture has chosen a dragon to be his coat of arms.

1 Design a **coat of arms** for a person named **Kingsnorth**.
Use pictures of things that sound like parts of this name.
Make sure you use bright colours and a bold design.

2 Design a **coat of arms** for yourself.
You might like to use pictures of things that sound like parts of your name.
You might like to use pictures of things that you like doing.

Amazing buildings

This page is from a factfinder book about the wonders of the world.

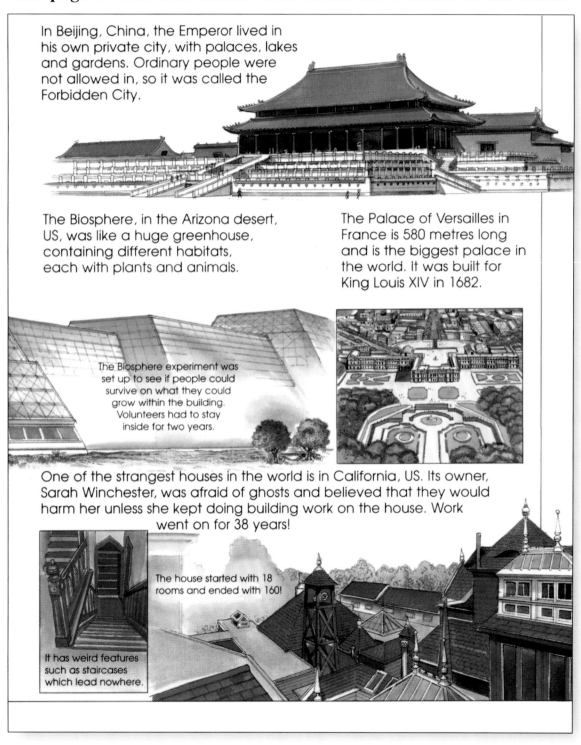

In Beijing, China, the Emperor lived in his own private city, with palaces, lakes and gardens. Ordinary people were not allowed in, so it was called the Forbidden City.

The Biosphere, in the Arizona desert, US, was like a huge greenhouse, containing different habitats, each with plants and animals.

The Palace of Versailles in France is 580 metres long and is the biggest palace in the world. It was built for King Louis XIV in 1682.

The Biosphere experiment was set up to see if people could survive on what they could grow within the building. Volunteers had to stay inside for two years.

One of the strangest houses in the world is in California, US. Its owner, Sarah Winchester, was afraid of ghosts and believed that they would harm her unless she kept doing building work on the house. Work went on for 38 years!

The house started with 18 rooms and ended with 160!

It has weird features such as staircases which lead nowhere.

1 Who lived in the Forbidden City?

2 Who wasn't allowed in the Forbidden City?

3 Who lived in the Palace of Versailles?

4 Why did Sarah Winchester keep on adding new parts to her house?

5 a) Would you have preferred to have lived in The Forbidden City, The Palace at Versailles, or in Sarah Winchester's house?

  b) Give a good reason explaining why you chose this place to live.

1 Where did the Biosphere people get their food from?

2 Why do you think they built the Biosphere in the middle of a desert?

3 Why did the Biosphere have to be so big?

4 Which one of all the buildings on this page do you think was the most **useful**? Give a good reason for your answer.

5 Which one of the buildings on this page do you think was the most **useless**? Give a good reason for your answer.

An Alien Spaceship lands outside your school. The Aliens are friendly. They want to learn all about how different people live on Planet Earth. They can't stay long so they ask you to make them a **guidebook**.

They want to be guided to:
a) The home of a very rich person.
b) A very unusual home.
c) The home of a child.

If possible they want to know **where** these three places are, **what** they have inside them, **why** they are built the way they are, **when** they were built, **how** they were made (this might include the different materials they were made out of), and **who** lives, or lived, in them.

Make a separate page for each of the three places. Use the information on the opposite page for a and b. Use your own home for c.

Walt Disney

This entry from an encyclopedia is a biography, giving a brief life history of the famous film producer.

Disney, Walter Elias (1901–66)

Walt Disney was an American artist and film producer. His best-known films are the cartoons for which he created characters such as Mickey Mouse, Donald Duck and Pluto. Disney was born in the city of Chicago. In 1923 he made the world's first successful cartoon film, *Oswald the Rabbit*, but it was Mickey Mouse, who first appeared in 1928, that made cartoons really popular. The first Mickey Mouse movie was made in black and white; Disney's first colour cartoon was *Snow White and the Seven Dwarfs* (1937). Several successful films followed, many of which are still regularly shown, including *Bambi, Dumbo* and *Pinocchio*. In the 1940s Disney began making colour nature films (which won several Academy Awards, or 'Oscars') and feature films for children such as *Treasure Island*, and *Mary Poppins*, in which cartoons and live actors are combined.

Mickey Mouse, the cartoon creation of Walt Disney.

1 In which city was Walt Disney born?

2 In which country was Walt Disney born?

3 What sort of films was Walt Disney most famous for making?

4 What sort of animal starred in Walt Disney's **first** successful cartoon?

5 How was *Snow White and the Seven Dwarfs* different to the cartoons Disney had made earlier in his career?

1 What is the nickname given to Academy Awards?

2 What sort of films made by Disney were given Academy Awards?

3 What was unusual about the film *Mary Poppins*?

4 Why do you think the people who made this encyclopedia put a picture of Mickey Mouse underneath the information about Walt Disney?

5 Make a list that shows:
   a) One Walt Disney film from the 1920s.
   b) One Walt Disney film from the 1930s.
   c) Four cartoon characters invented by Walt Disney.

Write a short biography of **yourself**, to be included in an encyclopedia about everyone in your school.

Try to include when and where you were born, where you live now and what you like doing. Make sure you tell the readers what you are well-known for at your school.

Jamaican music

This page is from a round-the-world songbook.

A guiro is a hollow wooden instrument with lots of ridges. You scrape it with a stick. This makes a dry, rasping sound.

Here are some of the percussion instruments which are used in Jamaican music.

Congas are tall drums which you usually play with your fingers or the palms of your hands.

Don't know why you went away,
Water come a me eye.
When you comin' home to stay?
Water come a me eye.
Come back, Liza, come back girl,
Water come a me eye.
Come back, Liza, come back girl,
Water come a me eye.

Maracas have a hollow case filled with seeds or beads which rattle when you shake them.

Steel pans are metal drums which are often played in bands. The tops are divided into separate sections. Each section makes a different note when you hit it.

Larger pans accompany the tunes. They play lower notes, and help to make a strong rhythm.

Soprano (or ping pong) pans are the smallest pans. They usually play 25 different notes, and are used to play the tunes in a band.

There are often other drums and percussion instruments in steel bands, as well as the pans.

A

1 What do you use to play a **guiro**?

2 What do you use to play the **congas**?

3 What makes the rattling noise inside **maracas**?

4 What are the **pans** made from?

5 Look carefully at the picture at the bottom of the page. Why do you think **ping pong pans** are good instruments to play in processions and carnivals?

B

1 Look carefully at the words of the song in the middle of the page. What do you think **water come a me eye** means?

2 **a)** How do you think the singer of the song is feeling?
   b) What has happened to make the singer feel like this?
   c) What does the singer say will make things better?

3 **a)** Look carefully at the picture at the bottom of the page. Do you think the band is playing the same song that appears in the middle of the page?
   b) Give a good reason to explain your answer.

4 **a)** Which **one** of the instruments on the opposite page would you like to play?
   b) Give a good reason to explain why you would choose this one.

C

1 Think of a good **title** for the song that appears on the opposite page.

2 Think of a good **name** for the band that appears in the picture.

3 Now try writing a new song for a steel band, following the repeating style of the song opposite.

What am I?

These little puzzles are called riddles, and come from an old book of nursery rhymes. The pictures next to the riddles give clues to the answers.

Two legs sat upon three legs
With one leg in his lap;
In comes four legs
And runs away with one leg;
Up jumps two legs,
Catches up three legs,
Throws it after four legs,
And makes him bring back one leg.

In marble walls as white as milk,
Lined with a skin as soft as silk,
Within a fountain crystal-clear,
A golden apple doth appear.
No doors there are to this stronghold,
Yet thieves break in and steal the gold.

Little Nancy Etticoat,
With a white petticoat,
And a red nose;
She has no feet or hands,
The longer she stands
The shorter she grows.

As round as an apple,
As deep as a cup,
And all the king's horses
Cannot pull it up.

1 In the first riddle who or what is **two legs**?

2 In the first riddle who or what is **four legs**?

3 In the first riddle who or what is **three legs**?

4 a) In the first riddle what is the first thing **two legs** does with **three legs**?
  b) In the first riddle what is the second thing **two legs** does with **three legs**?

The answer to the second riddle is **an egg**.

1 a) What is the golden apple inside the egg?
  b) Give a reason that explains how this part of the egg is like an apple.

2 a) What part of the egg is the **marble walls**?
  b) What part of the egg is the **fountain**?

3 a) Who are the thieves who break into the egg?
  b) What does it mean when it says the thieves **steal the gold**?

4 a) What is **Nancy Etticoat**?
  b) Explain clearly how **The longer she stands**
  The shorter she grows.

5 What is the answer to the fourth riddle?

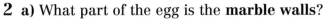

shell — white
yolk

Here are two more riddles, and their answers, all muddled up together.

One of these riddles is three lines long and one is four lines long, and both of them rhyme.

Sort them out, write them down, and draw a picture to show the answer.

She leaves a bit of her tail in a trap.

Oh, whatever can that be?

Higher than a house,

And a long tail which she can let fly,

Old Mother Twitchett has only one eye

Higher than a tree

And every time she goes over a gap,

A star   A needle   and   thread

Good Taste

This poem looks, in tiny detail, at an extraordinary moment in a man's life.

Good Taste

Travelling, a man met a tiger, so . . .
He ran. The tiger ran after him
Thinking: How fast I run . . . But

The road thought: How long I am . . . Then
They came to a cliff, yes, the man
Grabbed at an ash root and swung down

Over its edge. Above his knuckles, the tiger.
At the foot of the cliff, its mate. Two mice,
One black, one white, began to gnaw the root.

And by the traveller's head grew one
Juicy strawberry, so . . . hugging the root
The man reached out and plucked the fruit.

How sweet it tasted!

Christopher Logue

A

1 Why did the man have to start running?

2 What stopped the man running any further?

3 How did the man get over the edge of the cliff without hurting himself?

4 What danger was waiting at the **bottom** of the cliff?

5 Why were the mice a danger to the man?

6 What was the **one** good thing about the man's position?

B

1 Why does the strawberry taste so good?

2 Choose **three** of the words below which best describe the traveller.

lucky   unlucky   brave   thankful   strong   greedy   silly   sensible

Copy down the three words and beside each one explain why you have chosen it.

3 Poems often carry a message. What do you think the poet is trying to tell you in this poem?

4 What do you think will happen to the man?

C

This poem is short, but a great many things happen, one after another!

The traveller meets the tiger ... the tiger chases the man... the man goes over the cliff...the mice appear... the traveller eats the strawberry.

To keep the poem fast and exciting the poet uses phrases full of short words like: **a man met a tiger, One white, one black, How fast I am, How long I am, He ran.**

The poet also uses lots of commas and lots of joining words like **so, But, Then,** and **yes**.

Using the same sort of words write an exciting adventure poem of your own. Don't use more than 12 lines.

Call it: **The wolves go hunting**.

Stopping by Woods

Robert Frost was an American poet, writing earlier this century.

STOPPING BY WOODS ON A SNOWY EVENING

Whose woods these are I think I know.
His house is in the village though;
He will not see me stopping here
To watch his woods fill up with snow.

My little horse must think it queer
To stop without a farmhouse near
Between the woods and frozen lake
The darkest evening of the year.

He gives his harness bells a shake
To ask if there is some mistake.
The only other sound's the sweep
Of easy wind and downy flake.

The woods are lovely, dark and deep,
But I have promises to keep,
And miles to go before I sleep,
And miles to go before I sleep.

ROBERT FROST

A

1 What reason does the poet give in the first verse for stopping in the woods?

2 Why won't the owner of the woods see the poet?

3 How did the poet reach the woods?

4 Write down the word in the second verse that tells you it is very cold.

5 Write down **two** sounds that break the silence of the woods.

B

1 Write down three things the poet likes about the woods.

2 Why is the horse surprised when they stop by the woods?

3 The poet describes the wind as an **easy** wind. What does the word **easy** tell you about the way the wind is blowing?

4 Write down the words used in the poem that tell you the poet is on a long journey.

5 Why is the poet going on this journey?

6 What do you think the poet would like to do most of all?

C

When Robert Frost wrote this poem he made sure the first three verses followed a pattern.

Each verse had four lines.

Each line had eight syllables.

The first, second and fourth line of each verse rhymed.

The third line of each verse rhymed with the first line of the next verse.

Using the same pattern write two verses of your own.

Write about:

Walking to school on a rainy morning.

Storytime

This poem tells about a very unusual day at school.

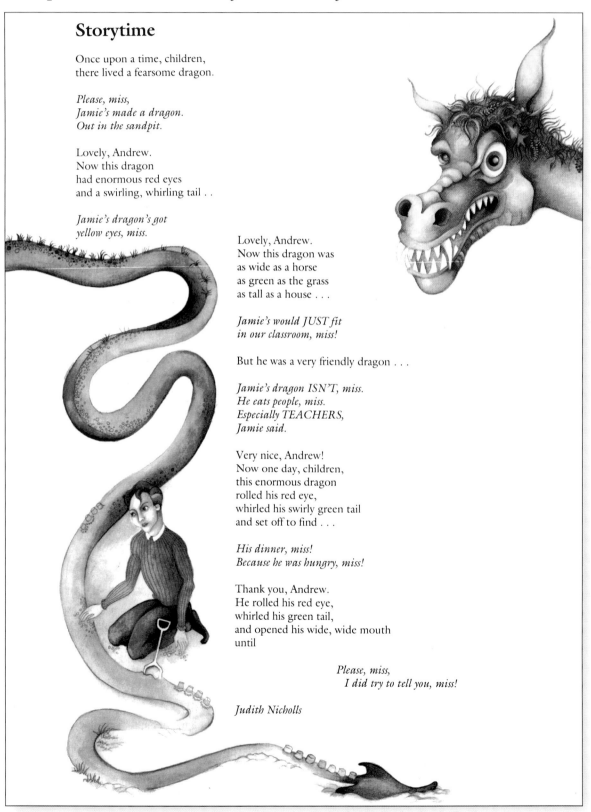

Storytime

Once upon a time, children,
there lived a fearsome dragon.

Please, miss,
Jamie's made a dragon.
Out in the sandpit.

Lovely, Andrew.
Now this dragon
had enormous red eyes
and a swirling, whirling tail . .

Jamie's dragon's got
yellow eyes, miss.

Lovely, Andrew.
Now this dragon was
as wide as a horse
as green as the grass
as tall as a house . . .

Jamie's would JUST fit
in our classroom, miss!

But he was a very friendly dragon . . .

Jamie's dragon ISN'T, miss.
He eats people, miss.
Especially TEACHERS,
Jamie said.

Very nice, Andrew!
Now one day, children,
this enormous dragon
rolled his red eye,
whirled his swirly green tail
and set off to find . . .

His dinner, miss!
Because he was hungry, miss!

Thank you, Andrew.
He rolled his red eye,
whirled his green tail,
and opened his wide, wide mouth
until

          Please, miss,
            I did try to tell you, miss!

Judith Nicholls

A

1 There are two people talking in the poem. Who is speaking at the very beginning of the poem?

2 What is this person trying to do?

3 What is the name of the person who keeps interrupting?

4 **a)** Who has been playing in the sandpit?
   b) What has this person made in the sandpit?

5 What happens at the end of the poem?

B

1 How can you tell that the sandpit is very big?

2 What is the **main** difference between the dragon in the teacher's book and Jamie's dragon?

3 Write down the words you think the teacher is reading out when Andrew sees the dragon coming in.

4 Why are some of the words Andrew says written in capital letters?

5 Did you enjoy reading this poem? Explain as fully as you can why you liked, or disliked, the poem.

C

The poem doesn't explain how the dragon came to life.

Perhaps some of the children made up a **spell** that made it come alive.

Spells often rhyme.

Part of a spell is printed below. If you take the first letter of each line and read downwards it spells **DRAGON**. The first line rhymes with the second line. Finish the spell. Make sure the third line rhymes with the fourth line and the fifth line rhymes with the sixth line.

Dangerous teeth and deadly roar,
Run in through our classroom door,
A
G
O
N

Conversation

This is a poem with two people talking.

Conversation

Why are you always tagging on?
You ought to be dressing dolls
Like other sisters.

Dolls! You know I don't like them.
Cold, stiff things lying so still.
Let's go to the woods and climb trees.
The crooked elm is the best.
From the top you can see the river
And the old man hills,
Hump-backed and hungry
As ragged beggars.
In the day they seem small and far away
But at night they crowd closer
And stand like frowning giants.
Come on! What are you waiting for?

I have better things to do.

It's wild in the woods today.
Rooks claw the air with their cackling.
The trees creak and sigh.
They say that long ago, slow Sam the woodcutter
Who liked to sleep in the hollow oak,
Was found dead there.
The sighing is his ghost, crying to come back.
Let's go and hear it.

I hate the sound.

You mean you're afraid?

Of course not.
Jim and I are going fishing.

Can I come too?

What do you know about fishing?
You're only a girl.

OLIVE DOVE

42

A

1 Why is the boy fed up with his sister?

2 What does the girl dislike?

3 Where does the girl want to go to?

4 What does she want to do when she gets there?

5 How can you tell the girl has been there before?

B

1 Find **two** words the poet uses to describe the sounds the trees make.

2 What does the girl say is causing these sounds?

3 **a)** What does the girl's brother say when she says they should go and listen to this sound?

   b) What do you think this tells us about the boy?

4 What excuse does the brother give to explain why he can't go with her?

5 Why do you think the boy doesn't want his sister to go fishing with him?

6 Why do you think the girl prefers trees to dolls?

7 The girl calls the hills **frowning giants**. What do you think this tells you about how she sees the hills?

C

The girl in the poem always seems to be looking for excitement.

She wants to go to the wild, haunted wood. She thinks the hills are alive.

Her brother seems to be more cautious.

Imagine she **did** go fishing.

Write down a continuation of the **conversation**, about how the girl sees the riverbank, and how the boy sees it.

What has happened to Lulu?

In this poem a child has woken up to find another member of the family has gone away in the night.

What has happened,to Lulu, mother?
    What has happened to Lu?
There's nothing in her bed but an old rag-doll
    And by its side a shoe.

Why is her window wide, mother,
    The curtain flapping free,
And only a circle on the dusty shelf
    Where her money-box used to be?

Why do you turn your head, mother,
    And why do the tear-drops fall?
And why do you crumple that note on the fire
    And say it is nothing at all?

I woke to voices late last night,
    I heard an engine roar,
Why do you tell me the things I heard
    Were a dream and nothing more?

I heard somebody cry, mother,
    In anger or in pain,
But now I ask you why, mother,
    You say it was a gust of rain.

Why do you wander about as though
    You don't know what to do?
What has happened to Lulu, mother?
    What has happened to Lu?

Charles Causley

A

1 What has Lulu left behind?

2 How do you think Lulu got out of the house?

3 What did Lulu take with her?

4 How can you tell Lulu's mother is sad that Lulu has gone?

5 List **two** sounds the child heard in the night.

B

Evidence indicates that something has happened.

1 What evidence is there in the poem that Lulu left quickly?

2 What evidence is there in the poem that Lulu left a message behind to explain why she has gone?

3 What evidence is there in the poem that someone was helping Lulu get away once she had left the house?

4 **a)** Who do you think gave a cry in the middle of the night?
  b) Why do you think this person made this cry?

5 Read the poem again carefully. Think about all the evidence. Why do you think Lulu left the house?

C

The child talking in this poem asks many questions, but receives no answers.

Write a final verse for the poem.

Make sure it follows the same pattern as the other verses.

Make sure it has four lines.

Make the first and third lines longer than the second and fourth lines.

Make the second line rhyme with the fourth line.

In your verse make Lulu's mother explain why Lulu has gone away.

A Smuggler's Song

This poem is about the smugglers who, over two hundred years ago, used to cross from France to the south of England in small sailing boats. They brought with them tobacco and brandy. Anyone bringing tobacco and brandy into the country was supposed to pay a tax to the customs officers. The smugglers didn't want to pay the tax so they brought their cargo in secretly, at night. This poem is telling a young girl what she should do if she hears strange sounds.

If you wake at midnight, and hear a horse's feet,
Don't go drawing back the blind, or looking in the street,
Them that asks no questions isn't told a lie.
Watch the wall, my darling, while the Gentlemen go by!
    Five and twenty ponies
    Trotting through the dark –
    Brandy for the Parson,
    'Baccy for the Clerk;
    Laces for a lady, letters for a spy,
And watch the wall, my darling, while the Gentlemen go by!

Running round the woodlump if you chance to find
Little barrels, roped and tarred, all full of brandy-wine,
Don't you shout to come and look, nor use 'em for your play.
Put the brushwood back again – and they'll be gone next day!

If you see the stable-door setting open wide;
If you see a tired horse lying down inside;
If your mother mends a coat cut about and tore;
If the lining's wet and warm – don't you ask no more!

If you meet King George's men, dressed in blue and red,
You be careful what you say, and mindful what is said.
If they call you 'pretty maid', and chuck you 'neath the chin,
Don't you tell where no one is, nor yet where no one's been!

Knocks and footsteps round the house – whistles after dark –
You've no call for running out till the house-dogs bark,
Trusty's here, and *Pincher's* here, and see how dumb they lie –
They don't fret to follow when the Gentlemen go by!

Rudyard Kipling

A

1 What sound might wake the girl at midnight?

2 Who are the 'Gentlemen'?

3 Name two other things, apart from tobacco and brandy, that the smugglers sometimes bring with them.

4 What sort of container is the brandy carried in?

5 What do the smugglers use to cover up the brandy so that it can't be seen?

6 What do the smugglers use to transport the brandy from the seashore to the towns where they sell it?

7 Read the introduction carefully and then read the fourth verse. Who do you think **King George's Men** might be?

8 What reward might the girl be given if she does as she is told?

B

1 What do you think made the **cuts** in the coat that appears in verse three?

2 What do you think made the lining of the coat **wet** and **warm**?

3 Who do you think the **tired horse** belongs to?

4 What do King George's men want the girl to tell them?

5 How will King George's men try to make the girl tell them what they want to know?

C

Use the information in the poem to write a story about smugglers.

Imagine you lived in the days of the smugglers. You wake one night at midnight and you hear the clatter of horses' hooves. You decide you **will** look out into the street!

You see the smugglers and they see you!

What happens next? Do you help them with the ponies and the brandy? Do King George's men come after you? Do you have to find a place to hide? Do you sail across to France?

Perseus and the Gorgons

This is part of a myth from ancient Greece.

At last Perseus found the Gorgons. They were asleep among the rocks, and Perseus was able to look at them safely.

Although they were asleep, the live serpents which formed their hair were writhing venomously. The sight filled Perseus with horror. How could he get near enough without being turned to stone?

Suddenly Perseus knew what to do. He now understood why Athena had given him the shining bronze shield. Looking into it he saw clearly the reflection of the Gorgons. Using the shield as a mirror, he crept forward. Then with a single swift blow he cut off the head of the nearest Gorgon. Her name was Medusa.

In one mighty swoop, Perseus grabbed the head of Medusa. He placed it safely in his bag and sprang into the air on his winged sandals.

A

1 What were the Gorgons doing when Perseus found them?

2 What was unusual about the Gorgons' hair?

3 What would happen to Perseus if the Gorgons looked into his eyes?

4 Why had Perseus brought a bag with him?

5 What happened to Medusa?

6 Look at the picture. Why do you think Perseus needed to have sandals with wings on?

B

1 Who had given Perseus his shield?

2 How did Perseus look at the Gorgons without them looking at him?

3 Why do you think the Gorgons had snakes for hair?

4 Write down the word used in the **third** paragraph that tells you Perseus moved very carefully towards the Gorgons.

5 Write down the word used in the **second** paragraph that means **wriggling**.

6 Using two or three sentences write down what you think happens immediately after Perseus flies into the air on his winged sandals.

C

Myths are old stories that tell us amazing tales about the heroes and gods who walked the Earth in ancient times.

In **myths** people who do wrong are often punished by being turned into monsters.

The **Gorgons** were once three sisters. They were turned into the monsters you can see in the picture.

Write the story that explains **why** these three sisters were turned into such dreadful creatures. What had they done to be punished in this way? Why were they given snakes for hair and the power to turn people into stone?

The first ox

This page is about a Chinese myth on how the ox came to Earth.

THE ORIGIN OF THE OX

THE SAGE'S MOUNT
The renowned Chinese sage Lao-Tzu, founder of Taoism, one of China's religions, began his wanderings riding upon an ox, as shown in this bronze.

❖

THE OX
The ox has a special place in Chinese myth. It is the second sign of the zodiac; people born under this sign are thought to be reliable and considerate. At various times in history, the ox has been protected by law. Many Chinese still feel that eating beef is a shameful way to repay an animal that puts its strength at the service of humans.

LONG AGO, LIFE was very hard – even harder than it is today. People had to struggle in the fields with their bare hands to grow enough food to feed themselves. They rarely had enough to eat – even though they worked day and night.

The Emperor of Heaven saw the poor people toiling on the earth and took pity on them. He summoned the Ox star from the sky, and sent it down to tell the people that if they worked hard, they would be able to eat well every third day.

The Ox rushed down to pass on the news. But it was a stupid creature, and so proud of being the Emperor's messenger, that it muddled the message. The Ox told the people that if they worked hard the Emperor of Heaven said they could have three meals a day!

The Emperor of Heaven did not want the people on earth

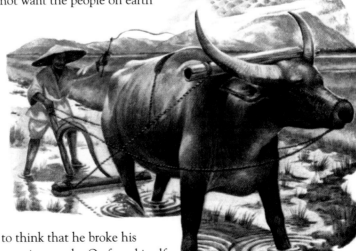

The Emperor of Heaven

to think that he broke his promises, so the Ox found itself yoked to the plough to till the fields. People just couldn't have done the work by themselves.

The Ox finds itself yoked to the plough to help mankind till the fields

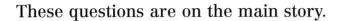

These questions are on the main story.

1 Which country does this story come from?

2 What did the people on Earth spend almost all their time doing?

3 Who decided the people on Earth needed to be encouraged?

4 Write down the message the Ox was **supposed** to bring.

5 Write down the message the Ox **did** bring.

6 How did the Ox help the people of Earth?

7 Why do you think the Ox was better at this job than the people on Earth?

8 **a)** Do you think it was fair that the Ox had to help the people on Earth?
   b) Give a good reason to support your answer.

These questions are on the information at the side of the page.

1 Name one of China's religions.

2 How else did people use oxen?

3 How can you tell that the Chinese people valued and respected the ox?

4 Why do you think people born under the sign of the Ox are thought to be **considerate**? (Considerate means wanting to help others.)

In the story on the opposite page the Ox appears to be rather stupid. Because he muddles up one message he has to spend the rest of his life doing a hard, tiring and dirty job.

One day, however, the Emperor of Heaven, takes pity on the Ox.

For one day only the Emperor allows the Ox three wishes.

What three wishes do you think the Ox would make?

What would he want to do?

How would he spend his holiday?

Write the story of **The Ox and his Three Wishes**.

The Wind in the Willows

These pages are part of the famous book by Kenneth Grahame, first published in 1908.

There was nothing to alarm him at first. Twigs crackled under his feet, logs tripped him, funguses on stumps startled him for a moment, but that was all fun, and exciting.

Then the faces began.

He thought he saw a little evil face, looking out at him from a hole. He quickened his pace, telling himself cheerfully not to begin imagining things, or there would be simply no end to it. He passed another hole, and another; and then – yes! – no! – yes! certainly a little narrow face flashed up and was gone. He hesitated – and strode on. Then suddenly there were hundreds of them, coming and going rapidly, all hard-eyed and evil and sharp.

Then the whistling began.

Very faint and shrill it was, and far behind him, when first he heard it.

Then it broke out on either side. They were up and alert and ready, whoever they were! And he was alone, and far from help and the night was closing in.

Then the pattering began.

Was it in front or behind? It seemed to be closing in on him, hunting, chasing something or – somebody? In panic, he began to run too. He ran up against things, he fell over things and into things. At last he took refuge in the deep dark hollow of an old beech tree.

He was too tired to run any further and could only snuggle down into the dry leaves and hope he was safe.

Meantime the Rat, warm and comfortable, dozed by his fireside. Then a coal slipped, the fire crackled and he woke with a start. He reached down to the floor for his verses, and then looked

round for the Mole to ask him if he knew a rhyme for something or other. But the Mole was not there. He called "Moly!" several times, and, receiving no answer, got up and went out into the hall. The Mole's cap and goloshes were gone.

The Rat left the house hoping to find the Mole's tracks. There they were, sure enough. He could see the imprints in the mud, leading direct to the Wild Wood. The Rat looked very grave.

A

1 At first the Mole was having fun. What was the first thing he saw that **really** frightened him?

2 What was the first **sound** that really frightened Mole?

3 What do you think was making the **pattering** noise?

4 What time of day was it when the Mole thought he was being followed?

5 Give **two** reasons why the Mole went into the hollow tree.

B

1 What made the Rat wake up?

2 What had the Rat been doing **before** he fell asleep?

3 Write down the words that tell you the Rat was expecting the Mole to be nearby.

4 What was the first clue the Rat had that the Mole had gone out?

5 What made the Rat sure that the Mole had gone out?

6 **Grave** in the last line means **worried**. Why do you think the Rat was worried?

7 Do you think the Rat was right or wrong to be worried? Give a good reason to back up your answer.

8 Find a word in the story that means **slept**.

C

The writer of this story uses **contrast** to make us feel how miserable the Mole must be.

Contrast is when the writer compares two very different things.

To begin with the writer describes how lonely and frightened Mole is in the cold and snowy Wild Wood. Then the writer describes how cosy and comfortable the Rat is in his warm house. Because the Rat is having such a good time it makes us feel how horrible it must be for the Mole.

Write a **contrast** that compares the life of a pet goldfish to the life led by a fish in the sea; or else of a pet mouse compared with a field mouse.

The chicken's tale

This is a chapter from a longer story, by Anne Fine. A chicken is telling the amazing story of how she escaped from the farm where she had lived all her life.

It was a wet and windy night, so wet you could slip and drown, so windy no one would hear your cries. Only a snake or a toad would choose to be away from shelter on such a night. And that is why only the snakes and the toads saw the gleaming green light pouring down from the black sky.

We chickens saw nothing, of course. How could we? There are no windows in the chicken shed. If we had windows, our lives could not be ruled so well by the electric light that decides when we wake and when we sleep and when we lay our eggs. After – oh, yes, of course, *after* – some of the hens in the cages by the door said that they'd heard the soft hum of the engines over the howling of the wind. But the rest of us think they were boasting. On that black night, the spaceship landed without a sound. And it was not until the shed door flew open, flooding us with an eerie green light, that most of us chickens woke with a flutter and a squawk.

Little green men.

And they spoke perfect Chicken. (Later we found out they spoke Pig and Cow and Crow and pretty well everything. It's one of the ways in which they are, as they put it, 'superior'. They can speak any language they happen to meet. But on that first night we were amazed that they spoke perfect Chicken.)

Not that they were polite with it.

'Chickens!' said the spindliest and greenest, and it was almost like a groan. 'Travel a frillion miles, and what do you find when you arrive? A chicken!'

The others flicked the catches of our cage doors with their willowy green fingers.

'Out, out!' they called. 'Wakey, wakey! Make room! Out you get! Clear off! Go and make your own nests! The party's over!'

The party's over? We chickens couldn't believe our luck. We'd been locked in those cages almost since we were born. Nothing to do. You can't even stretch your wings. You just stand there on a wire rack (*ruining* your feet) for your whole life. And the one thing they want you to do – laying your egg – you'd far rather do in private.

The party's over! I can't describe to you the din as we all fluttered clumsily down, and scrambled unsteadily for the door.

The little green men were even ruder now.

'Call themselves chickens? I've seen finer specimens on other planets begging to be put down!'

'Look at them! Twisted feet. Bare patches all over. And look at their beaks!'

'Disgusting!'

'Leave the door open as you go, please. This shed needs some fresh air.'

Fresh air! And we were out in it for the first time in our lives. We weren't going to hang around shutting the shed door. No fear. We were away. The last I heard as I went hobbling off on my poor feet into the night was one of the little green men scolding the stragglers.

'Hurry up. Out of those cages, *please*! We need them for others.'

With one last shudder and a flutter, I was off.

A

1 Why were there so few animals outside on the night the aliens came?

2 Why couldn't the chickens see the strange light in the sky?

3 Why couldn't the engine of the spaceship be heard?

4 How many miles do the aliens say they have travelled?

5 Give **one** reason why the chickens didn't like living in the cages.

B

1 Write down what one of the little green men said that tells you they were hoping to find creatures on Earth that were more exciting than chickens.

2 The chicken telling the story says that the aliens were "superior". She means that the aliens were able to do many more things than chickens or humans could do. What do you think is the most useful thing the aliens can do?

3 Why did the chickens have twisted feet?

4 Find **two** words in the story that describe how the chickens moved when they were let out of the cages for the first time.

5 Why were the chickens so keen to get outside?

6 The aliens say they need the cages. What do you think they are going to use the cages for?

C

The chicken tells the story from her point of view.

The chicken and her friends are really pleased to be able to escape.

The aliens, though, seem more interested in getting the chickens out of the way. They even seem to think the chickens are enjoying themselves!

Tell the same story from the point of view of the aliens.

Write your story like a **report**. Imagine you are the alien in charge of moving the chickens. You are sending a **report** back to your home planet explaining exactly what you have done. Make sure your report includes when you landed, where you landed, how you released the chickens, why you released the chickens and what you are planning to use their cages for now.

The Knee-High Man

This is a story by Julius Lester which has a strong moral lesson to it.

Once upon a time there was a knee-high man. He was no taller than a person's knees. Because he was so short, he was very unhappy. He wanted to be big like everybody else.

One day he decided to ask the biggest animal he could find how he could get big. So he went to see Mr Horse. 'Mr Horse, how can I get big like you?'

Mr Horse said, 'Well, eat a whole lot of corn. Then run around a lot. After a while you'll be as big as me.'

The knee-high man did just that. He ate so much corn that his stomach hurt. Then he ran and ran and ran until his legs hurt. But he didn't get any bigger. So he decided that Mr Horse had told him something wrong. He decided to go ask Mr Bull.

'Mr Bull? How can I get big like you?'

Mr Bull said, 'Eat a whole lot of grass. Then bellow and bellow as loud as you can. The first thing you know, you'll be as big as me.'

So the knee-high man ate a whole field of grass. That made his stomach hurt. He bellowed and bellowed and bellowed all day and all night. That made his throat hurt. But he didn't get any bigger. So he decided that Mr Bull was all wrong too.

Now he didn't know anyone else to ask. One night he heard Mr Hoot Owl hooting, and he remembered that Mr Owl knew everything.

'Mr Owl? How can I get big like Mr Horse and Mr Bull?'

'What do you want to be big for?' Mr Hoot Owl asked.

'I want to be big so that when I get into a fight, I can whip everybody,' the knee-high man said.

Mr Hoot Owl hooted. 'Anybody ever try to pick a fight with you?'

The knee-high man thought a minute. 'Well, now that you mention it, nobody ever did try to start a fight with me.'

Mr Owl said, 'Well, you don't have any reason to fight. Therefore, you don't have any reason to be bigger than you are.'

'But, Mr Owl,' the knee-high man said, 'I want to be big so I can see far into the distance.'

Mr Hoot Owl hooted. 'If you climb a tall tree, you can see into the distance from the top.'

The knee-high man was quiet for a minute. 'Well, I hadn't thought of that.'

Mr Hoot Owl hooted again. 'And that's what's wrong, Mr Knee-High Man. You hadn't done any thinking at all. I'm smaller than you, and you don't see me worrying about being big. Mr Knee-High Man, you wanted something that you didn't need.'

A

1 Why was the knee-high man so unhappy?

2 Why did the knee-high man ask the Horse for help?

3 What were the **two** pieces of advice the Horse gave the knee-high man?

4 Name **two** things that made the knee-high man's stomach hurt.

5 Why did the throat of the knee-high man hurt so much?

6 Why was the owl called Mr **Hoot** Owl?

B

1 The owl wasn't very big. Why did the knee-high man ask him for help?

2 **a)** What reason did the knee-high man give the Owl for wanting to be big?
  b) Explain why the Owl thought this was a silly reason.

3 **a)** What was the **second** reason the knee-high man gave to explain why he wanted to be big?
  b) How did the Owl say the knee-high man could solve that problem?

4 What does the Owl say the knee-high man should have done **before** he started trying to be bigger?

5 **a)** Write down the word used in the story that describes the noise bulls make.
  b) Write down the slang word used in the story by the knee-high man that means **beat**.

C

Think of a moral that you might want to pass on to your readers. Place that moral in the context of some animal characters, as with this story, and write out a plot which proves your moral.

Frankenstein

This is part of one of the most famous horror stories ever written. It was written 200 years ago by Mary Shelley. It tells how a scientist, Dr Frankenstein, sets out to discover the secret of life, but ends up making a monster.

In my laboratory I made a body. I bought or stole all the pieces of human body that I needed, and slowly and carefully, I put them all together.

I did not let anybody enter my laboratory or my flat while I was doing this awful work. I was afraid to tell anybody my terrible secret.

I had wanted to make a beautiful man, but the face of the creature was horrible. Its skin was thin and yellow, and its eyes were as yellow as its skin. Its long black hair and white teeth were almost beautiful, but the rest of the face was very ugly.

Its legs and arms were the right shape, but they were huge. I had to use big pieces because it was too difficult to join small pieces together. My creature was two and a half metres tall.

For a year I had worked to make this creature, but now it looked terrible and frightening. I almost decided to destroy it. But I could not. I had to know if I could put life into it.

I joined the body to the wires from my machine. More wires joined the machine to the mast. I was sure that my machine could use electricity from lightning to give life to the body. I watched and waited. Two days later I saw dark clouds in the sky, and I knew that a storm was coming. At about one o'clock in the morning the lightning came. My mast began to do its work immediately, and the electricity from the lightning travelled down the mast to my machine. Would the machine work?

At first nothing happened. But after a few minutes I saw the creature's body begin to move. Slowly, terribly, the body came alive. Its arms and legs began to move, and slowly it sat up.

1 Where did Dr Frankenstein do his work?

2 Dr Frankenstein used **two** different methods to gather together all the different body parts he needed. What were these two methods?

3 What was the lightning going to strike **first**?

4 What power was contained in the lightning?

5 What did this power have to travel along to reach the machine?

6 What was the machine connected to?

7 At what time did the lightning strike?

1 a) How big was the creature?
   b) Why did it end up being this size?

2 How long had Dr Frankenstein taken to create his monster?

3 Why wasn't Dr Frankenstein pleased with what he had done?

4 Why didn't Dr Frankenstein destroy the creature?

5 Why, at first, might Dr Frankenstein have thought the machine wasn't working?

Dr Frankenstein knows that he should not carry on with his experiment. However, he cannot bear to destroy the monster he has made. To his surprise the monster comes alive.

What happens next?

How does the monster **feel**?

Is the monster glad to be alive?

Does the monster blame Dr Frankenstein for making him so ugly and terrifying?

Does the monster treat Dr Frankenstein like a friend?

Does the monster treat Dr Frankenstein like an enemy?

Write the next chapter of the story.

Gellert

This is an old Welsh folk story, which tells the story of the dog Gellert. His name is remembered in the town called Beddgelert.

One day, Prince Llewellyn went hunting in Dovey forest. He was cross because his favourite hunting dog Gellert was nowhere to be seen, and even crosser when, without Gellert, the whole day went by without the huntsmen catching anything.

When it grew dark, Llewellyn and his men rode home. As they went into the stable-yard, the dog Gellert slunk out to meet them. His ears were flat against his head, his tail drooped, he cowered along the ground on his belly, and his muzzle and jaws were red with blood.

With a sinking heart, Llewellyn remembered his baby son, one year old. He'd been playing happily in his cradle when the huntsmen left. Llewellyn ran upstairs to the baby's bedroom, and the dog Gellert cringed after him.

The room was a shambles. The cradle was overturned, rugs and curtains were torn and scattered, and everywhere was stained with fresh blood. Llewellyn rounded on the dog. "You murdered my son!" he shouted, and in a single stroke drew his sword and stabbed Gellert to the heart.

The dog gave a last, dying whimper. There was an answering, gurgling laugh from under one of the torn-down curtains. Llewellyn snatched the curtain away, and found his baby son alive, playing happily with a handful of bricks.

Beside the baby was the blood-stained, torn body of a wolf. It had crept into the baby's bedroom in search of prey, and Gellert the hunting-dog had fought it and killed it to save his young master's life.

1 What was the first thing that made Llewellyn cross?

2 What was the second thing that made Llewellyn cross?

3 Write down **two** words from the second paragraph that describe the way Gellert moved when his master came home.

4 Write down the words from the story that show it was the evening when Llewellyn came home.

5 Why did Llewellyn think Gellert had done something wrong?

6 What did Llewellyn think Gellert had done?

7 How did Llewellyn punish Gellert?

8 What should Llewellyn have done before he punished Gellert?

1 Why couldn't Llewellyn see his baby when he first went into the bedroom?

2 What was the first clue Llewellyn had that the baby was alive?

3 How can you tell that the baby wasn't upset by what had happened?

4 What would have happened if Gellert hadn't stayed in the castle?

5 How do you think Llewellyn felt when he found his baby was safe?

So that everyone will remember how brave Gellert has been, Llewellyn orders a statue to be made. The statue will show Gellert fighting the wolf. Around the base of the statue there is space for 100 words.

Re-tell the story of Gellert and the wolf in no more than 100 words.

Make sure your story makes it clear how brave Gellert was, and how sad Llewellyn was when he found out the truth.

Pitichinella

This is a folk story from Italy, with a happy ending!

Pitichinella was a poor schoolgirl, an orphan. She was so poor that her house was a barrel in the village square, and she earned her food by getting up at half past four every morning and sweeping the church steps before the priest and people arrived for Mass.

One day, as she was sweeping, Pitichinella found a tiny copper coin among the dust. She ran to give it to the priest, but he smiled and said, "Keep it, my child, and welcome. Treat it as a gift from God, and make good use of it."

She bought a handful of lentils at the shop, and asked the shopkeeper's wife to look after them for her while she went to school. But the shopkeeper's wife left them unattended on the kitchen stool, and while her back was turned a cockerel stepped in from the yard and pecked up every one. "Oh Pitichinella," cried the shop-keeper's wife when Pitichinella came home from school that evening, "My cockerel's eaten all your lentils. Whatever shall we do?"

"Lentils, cockerel, cockerel, lentils," said Pitichinella. "I don't mind."

The shopkeeper's wife was so pleased with this answer that she gave Pitichinella the cockerel, and Pitichinella took it back to her barrel and tied it with a string round its leg to stop it straying in the night. Next morning she left it with Master Turidu while she went to school. But Turidu was a pig-farmer, and while his back was turned his prize porker snatched the cockerel and gobbled it down, feathers, beak, squawk and all. "Oh Pitichinella," cried Turidu when Pitichinella came home from school that evening, "My porker's eaten your cockerel. Whatever shall we do?"

"Cockerel, porker, porker, cockerel," said Pitichinella. "I don't mind."

Turidu was so delighted with this answer that he gave Pitichinella the porker, and Pitichinella took it back to the barrel and tied it with a string round its tail to stop it straying in the night. Next morning she left it with Bartolo the blacksmith while she went to school. But Bartolo was making a pair of wrought-iron doors for the police station, and while his back was turned one of his carriage-horses accidentally stamped on the porker and flattened it. "Oh Pitichinella," cried Bartolo when Pitichinella came home from school that evening, "My horse has flattened your porker. Whatever shall we do?"

"No problem," said Pitichinella. "Sell the horse, split the money and roast the porker for supper."

So that's what they did. And with her share of the money, Pitichinella bought a little whitewashed cottage, moved out of her barrel, and lived happily and prosperously from that day to this.

A

1 What did Pitichinella live in?

2 What do you think was the worst part of Pitichinella's job?

3 Why didn't Pitichinella buy an orange?

4 Why did Pitichinella buy lentils?

5 What happened to the lentils?

6 What job did Master Turidu do?

7 How did Pitichinella stop the cockerel from wandering off?

8 What job did Bartolo do?

9 What happened to the pig?

10 Why wasn't Pitichinella looking after the pig?

B

1 What does Pitichinella do at the start of the story that shows she is honest?

2 **a)** Would you have blamed Bartolo for what happened to the pig?
   b) Explain why you think the pig's accident was, or wasn't, Bartolo's fault.

3 What did Pitichinella do that shows you she hadn't grown fond of any of her animals?

4 **a)** Who do you think is the kindest person in the story?
   b) Give a good reason to explain why you have chosen this particular character from the story.

C

Pitichinella works hard and doesn't mind when something goes wrong. Because she doesn't make a fuss other people like her and help her. Invent another story about Pitichinella.

One day while Pitichinella is at school her cottage is picked up by a giant. The giant wants to give the cottage to his daughter so that she can use it as a dolls' house. Pitichinella doesn't make a fuss. She sets off to follow the giant and bring her cottage back. She follows his tracks to the entrance to a large cave. Sitting outside is a shepherd boy. He is crying. Continue the story.

Sources

The texts used in this book are extracted from the following full sources, and we are grateful for their permission to reproduce copyright material.

p 4 From *How do Bees Make Honey* by Anna Claybourne, © 1994 Usborne Publishing Ltd, reproduced by permission of Usborne Publishing.

p 6 'Hearing' from *What's Inside You* by Susan Meredith, © 1991 Usborne Publishing Ltd, reproduced by permission of Usborne Publishing.

p 8 From *Jump! Animals: Snakes* by Lucy Baker (Two-Can, 1990), Copyright © Two-Can Publishing Ltd 1990, reproduced by permission of the publisher. Photograph reproduced by permission of Zefa Pictures Ltd, The Stock Market.

p 10 From *Amazing Animal Records* by Su Swallow (Macdonald, 1981).

p 14 From *Starting Cooking* by Gill Harvey, © 1995 Usborne Publishing Ltd, reproduced by permission of Usborne Publishing.

p 16 Advertisement reproduced by permission of Dragons International.

p 18 Competition/advertisement from *Word Up*, August 1996, reproduced by permission of Dillons, the Bookstore. 'The Fidgiebray' by John Gethin reproduced by permission of John Gethin. 'The New Gnus' by John Foster, Copyright © John Foster, first published in John Foster (ed): *A Fifth Poetry Book* (OUP), reproduced by permission of the author. 'Dodo' by Jenny Morris, Copyright © Jenny Morris 1996, first published in *Crack Another Yolk*, reproduced by permission of the author. Cover of John Foster (ed): *Crack Another Yolk and Other Word Play Poems* (OUP, 1996), reproduced by permission of Oxford University Press. Cover of *Wondercrump Poetry!* (Red Fox, 1996) and 'It's rather dark in here' by Oliver Oldman reproduced by permission of Random House UK Ltd.

p 20 From *The Oxford Children's Pocket Book of Knowledge* (OUP, 1995), reproduced by permission of Oxford University Press.

p 22 Text from *What is Art?* by Rosemary Davidson (OUP, 1993), used by permission of Cynthia Parzych Publishing, Inc. BAL65827 'October: sowing the winter grain' by the Limbourg bothers, Très Riches Heures du Duc de Berry, (early 15th c), Victoria & Albert Museum, London/ Bridgeman Art Library, London, reproduced by permission of the Bridgeman Art Library.

p 24 From *Knights and Castles* by Judy Hindley, © 1993, 1976 Usborne Publishing Ltd, reproduced by permission of Usborne Publishing.

p 26 From *Heraldry* by J Brooke Little (Blackwell, 1975).

p 28 Text and Illustrations from *Wonders of the World* by Fiona Corbridge (Puffin Factfinders, 1996), Copyright © Zig Zag Publishing, 1996, reproduced by permission of Penguin Books Ltd.

p 30 From *Great Lives* by Simon Boughton (Kingfisher, 1988), Copyright © Grisewood & Dempsey Ltd 1988, reproduced by permission of Larousse PLC. Mickey Mouse image, © Disney, reproduced by permission of the Walt Disney Company Limited.

p 32 From *The Usborne Round the World Songbook* by Emma Danes, © 1995 Usborne Publishing Ltd, reproduced by permission of Usborne Publishing.

p 34 From *The Oxford Nursery Rhyme Book* by Peter and Iona Opie (OUP, 1955), reproduced by permission of Oxford University Press.

p 36 'Good Taste' by Christopher Logue from *Selected Poems* (Faber, 1995), reproduced by permission of the author and Faber & Faber Ltd.

p 38 'Stopping by Woods on a Snowy Evening' by Robert Frost from *The Poems of Robert Frost* edited by Edward Connery Lathem (Cape), reproduced by permission of the Estate of Robert Frost and Random House UK Ltd.

p 40 'Storytime' by Judith Nicholls from *The Midnight Forest and Other Poems* by Judith Nicholls, reproduced by permission of the publishers, Faber & Faber Ltd. Illustrated page from Michael Harrison and Christopher Stuart-Clark (eds): *The Oxford Book of Story Poems* (OUP, 1990), reproduced by permission of Oxford University Press.

p 42 'Conversation' by Olive Dove, first published in Paddy Bechely (ed): *Drumming in the Sky* (BBC, 1981), reprinted by permission of the author.

p 44 'What has happened to Lulu?' by Charles Causley from *Collected Poems for Children* (Macmillan), reproduced by permission of David Higham Associates. Illustrated page from Michael Harrison and Christopher Stuart-Clark (eds): *The Oxford Book of Story Poems* (OUP, 1990), reproduced by permission of Oxford University Press.

p 46 'A Smuggler's Song' by Rudyard Kipling from *Puck of Pook's Hill* (Macmillan, 1906), reproduced by permission of A P Watt Ltd on behalf of The National Trust.

p 48 'Perseus', text and illustration from *Famous Legends Book 1*, by J D M Preshous (1975), reproduced by permission of Ladybird Books Limited.

p 50 'The Origin of the Ox', text and illustration from *The Illustrated Book of Myths* by Neil Philip and Nilesh Mistry (Dorling Kindersley, 1995), reproduced by permission of the publishers.

p 52 Text and illustration from *The Wind in the Willows* by Kenneth Grahame, Copyright The University Chest, Oxford, reproduced by permission of Curtis Brown, London.

p 54 Text from *The Chicken's Tale* by Anne Fine (Methuen, 1992), reproduced by permission of Reed Books.

p 56 'Knee-High Man' from *The Knee-High Man and Other Tales* by Julius Lester, Copyright © 1972 by Julius Lester, reproduced by permission of Dial Books for Young Readers, a division of Penguin Books USA Inc. Illustrated page from Michael Harrison and Christopher Stuart-Clark (eds): The *Oxford Treasury of Children's Stories* (OUP, 1994), reproduced by permission of Oxford University Press.

p 58 From *Frankenstein* retold by Patrick Nobes (Oxford Bookworms, OUP, 1989), reproduced by permission of Oxford University Press. Illustration by Lynd Ward, The Bodleian Library.

p 60 'Gellert', text and illustration from *Tales of the British Isles, Wales* (Ginn, 1984) by Kenneth McLeish, reproduced by permission of Ginn & Company.

p 62 'Pitchinella', text and illustration from *Tales of the Mediterranean, Italy* (Ginn, 1986) by Kenneth McLeish, reproduced by permission of Ginn & Company.